8 Steps to a Winning Workers Compensation Program

A Workers' Compensation Guide for the Small to Medium Sized Employer

By

Gustavo L. Ortiz & Sean Patrick Nitzen

This book is available at a special discount when ordered in bulk quantities.

For information, contact G. Ortiz Productions & Publications at (949) 830-2027

ISBN 978-1-4303-0956-7

This publication is designed to provide accurate and authoritative information in regard to the subject matter covered. It is sold with the understanding that the publisher and authors are not engaged in rendering legal or other professional service. If legal advice or other expert assistance I required, the services of a competent professional should be sought

"Management is craftsmanship. Most of the time it is hard work to get a very few simple things across so that ordinary people can do them." –

Peter Drucker, Management expert

8 Steps to a Winning Workers Comp Program

A Workers' Compensation Guide
for the
Small to Medium Sized Employer

To our wives and families

Contents

Foreword

Workers Compensation, as we know it in America, is a little over a hundred years old. Although some would disagree, it was in fact an improvement for all the nation's workers' as the system became a no-fault system. As a result, employees now are assured of their employment after an industrial injury and are guaranteed the medical and financial assistance that was denied to workers at the turn of the last century. It is a system that was designed with good intentions. However, as with any no-fault benefit, there are those who seek to prosper at the expense of others and this, along with rising medical costs, growing litigation and the costs of corporate bureaucracy, we believe has in some instances literally placed workers compensation carriers in bankruptcy. On many occasions, the cost of workers compensation insurance has prevented many employers from doing business. It is with this in mind that we have developed these eight simple steps to help employers take control of their workers compensation costs; not just for the employer's sake, but for the workers for whom this system was originally devised.

Most risk management professionals believe that this subject should be approached more from a technical perspective. However, we have made it a practice to involve the employer and their employees from the beginning. Rather than create a comprehensive technical manual, we have chosen a different, more grass roots approach to refining your workers compensation program that will simplify the transfer of knowl-

1

edge to your staff and enable you to see concrete results. We suggest that you implement these changes over a course of time to enable appropriate indoctrination into your company's environment.

Sean & I have over 25 years of experience in workers compensation in the areas of claims administration, supervision, brokerage, investigation, vocational rehabilitation, workforce coaching and loss control. We expect after reading our book, that you will be empowered to implement these eight steps into your workers compensation program and soon see a return on your investment. We also expect that you will have a better understanding of the claims process and the personalities that you entrust your company to.

Overview of the Workers Comp System
Job Description — Claims Adjuster

One of the objectives for this book is to provide some insight into the claims profession with the goal of understanding one of the more thankless jobs in the insurance industry. Adjusting jobs vary from company to company, but one thing is for sure, it has been downgraded over the years. Claim adjusting was once a profession with all the requisites of a true white-collar job. The challenges of the job required an adjuster to be a quick and creative thinker; a skilled investigator; an astute negotiator; an empathetic counselor, but more importantly a claims adjuster had to be decisive in his actions.

The job has changed considerably over the years, especially with the introduction of computer automation. The skills an adjuster once required have been replaced by software programs that have taken the free thought and decision-making skills away from the position and have substituted technical reliance. The buzz-word coined in the late 80's typifying this transition was "paperless file". The vision was one of complete automation and the elimination of bulky files, automatic check dispersals, automated benefit notices and timely file review. However, whoever dreamed up the idea didn't take into consideration the fact that the insurance industry and the state governments were not prepared or equipped to embrace the new technology. Today, claims adjusters have become little more than data entry clerks; they rarely investigate; take statements;

gather evidence or provide impeccable customer service. This forces the insurance customer to choose either a proactive stance or a passive position. Most select the passive position, believing they are entitled to the impeccable service and commitment from the carrier they were promised when they signed on.

Theoretically, if a claims adjuster were lucky enough to handle a claim from inception to final resolution, the outcome would be favorable and expeditious. Through the religious use of a claims diary system an adjuster is supposed to address the many issues of a claim in a systematic and expeditious mode. But again, that's just in theory. The reality is that all the while the workers compensation system has been evolving and changing, the insurance industry has not. With the exception of newer web-based claims administration systems, the same industry workflow standards of 30 years ago remain the norm. This is to say, that claims adjusters still maintain caseloads between 170 to 200 cases, which are cases of varying difficulty. What that means to an employer is that their claims are being seen very infrequently as are their issues in the workplace. Because you are reading this book, you have chosen a proactive role of participation.

The Two Faces of Workers' Compensation — Defense vs. Applicant

There has always existed, this venerable fence we refer to when we try to guess which side a doctor's decision will favor. Is the doctor's final decision on the middle of the fence? Does it favor the employee? Does it favor the employer? When a case is not litigated we seek the middle of the fence; just a fair, objective opinion. However, the fence we are referring to, in a litigated case, divides the Applicant or Plaintiff side from the Defense side. Each side participates in activities to either diminish the ultimate exposure or value of the case, as is true on the side of the Defendant or to increase the value of the case, as is the case for the Applicant. The Applicant's side consists of the injured worker and his or her team of assigned specialists. The Defense side is the Employer/insurance Company and their team of chosen specialists. The term *"defense"* or *"defendant"* is meant to imply the employer in this publication. After all, it is the employer that must "defend" against the allegations brought forth by the applicant (injured employee). Each side, throughout the life of a Workers' Compensation claim, selfishly panders to their respective side. In California, the Applicant's side is widely considered to be the side for which the liberal construction of the Labor Code was written. The "defense" side is more conservative in nature. Ultimately, a workers' compensation claim is a combination of efforts made, discovery obtained and evidence gathered on both sides yet the insurance company and ultimately, the employer, pays for all product gathered on both sides. The only time both sides come together in what seems to be complete cooperation, is at the time of deposition and/or Agreed Medical Evaluation. At the time of the Deposition, the applicant's attorney and the defense attorney both agree on a date, time and place of a deposition. Will it be conducted at the applicant attorney's office or that of defense counsel? Who ever hosts this event is usually in charge of selecting the court reporter. All expenses, including fees payable to applicant's counsel for his or her time at this deposition, is paid by the employer through their workers compensation insurance policy.

Interestingly enough, by the time the case is heard at the Workers' Compensation Appeals Board, the attorney's representing each side, depending on their tenure in this industry, are as friendly as old college roommates. Each concedes their share as is expected and then pays a visit to the assigned judge. The judge will side in favor of the employee unless incontrovertible evidence is shown to effectively discredit the employee.

When you take into consideration all of the rules, procedures, disputes, delays, discretionary charges and patterns of practice that press upon the resolution of claims in the Workers Compensation Appeals process, it is obvious that the health and vocational future of the injured employee is no longer the priority.

The Players —
Doctors, Attorneys, Judges and Lien Claimants

Are there too many hands in the cookie jar? This industry is wrought with long standing alliances. If you know the identity of one party, say a much respected attorney providing applicant services over the past fifteen years or so, you have a better than fifty-fifty chance of guessing the primary treating physician, physical therapist provider, vocational rehabilitation counselor, interpreting company, subpoena company and pharmacy. According to one employer, it seems they travel in packs. They are well known to industry participants and have a well-oiled, tried and true game plan.

Experience cannot replace aggressiveness. Knowing the next four or five moves of these players can buy time and cut costs. In order to successfully minimize losses, the employer must have its own well-oiled machine. We'll share this with you in later chapters.

If you have never had a chance to see the California Workers' Compensation Appeals Board (WCAB) or your state's workers comp appeals system in action, make it a "must see" on your list of places to visit. Don't let the fact that "trials" take place there, or that an "appellate process" may be at work, intimidate you. You will not see Tom Cruise or Raymond Burr storm into the courtroom belching out "I want the truth!" This is more of an event under the Big Top than one of jurisprudence. Most of the discussions are very informal and uneventful. Most attorneys are at the WCAB on a few different cases on the same day and spend maybe three to five days or more a month there. On many occasions it is the first time an injured worker actually meets his or her attorney face to face. This is where witnesses and employer representatives sit in lunch rooms for the better part of the day just on a wild notion that your case will actually be heard. If we sound a bit disrespectful, we mean to be.

The appeals process is extremely antiquated and inefficient and over the years has transformed the way in which claims are pursued on your behalf. Defense attorneys no longer "defend"; they settle. Applicant attorneys no longer "appeal"; they, in many cases, extort. In some states like California the scales have been tipped a bit more to the employer side recently with the change in the permanent disability rating system and the introduction of the Medical Provider Network system. However, the remaining parties in these litigated cases still wait their turns to extract money from insurance carriers or self-insured employers, which is to say, they extract the money from *your* pocket. These are usually the doctor groups, translators, pharmacies and medical equipment suppliers who have all filed liens against a case with the expectation of receiving approximately 75% to 100%of the amounts they originally billed using a lien. There are many hands in the cookie jar and without proactive steps taken by the employer, these parties will remain unchecked.

The Liberal Construction of the Labor Code Stacked Against You

California is one of many liberal states and as such designed its workers compensation system to lay the burden of proof on the employer. There should be no question; the Labor Code will favor the injured worker. It must, as a no-fault system; it must ensure that injured workers receive the benefits they deserve. Most employers agree with this, however, as with any no-fault system, there exists an element of society that wishes to take advantage of the system. These individuals do so to a point of criminal intent. As a result the burden of proof just became heavier.

The mere allegation of an industrial injury is all it takes for you, the employer, to be placed on notice of a new and litigated, workers' compensation claim. You likely, will not have had even a clue that the employee in question had injured himself/herself on the job. It's very possible that an injury never occurred. But who's to say? In all likelihood the employee's claim will fall into one of four categories 1) a post-termination claim of injury 2) a claim of new and further injuries 3) a fraudulent claim of injury or 4) an accepted claim. The first three kinds of claims can be costly and must be handled aggressively by all parties. The reason for this is that in a workers compensation claim, the employee is given the benefit of the doubt and the employer is given the burden of proof. The challenges an employer faces are enhanced further by media promotion of attorney's services throughout the daytime hours, when disabled workers, the unemployed and recently laid off are home feeling, desperate, fearful or simply do not know if their employer will want them to return to work. This is where many of today's problems grow and where many weaknesses exist for employers. And while insurance companies are contractually obligated to "defend" the employer, time, resources and a deteriorating sense of customer service now prevents a proper defense. Attorneys representing your interests at the Appeals Board or trial are there to effectuate a settlement and nothing more. This leaves you with only one course of action.

Step 1

Become Proactive ...

By Insisting on Your Involvement

For the adjuster, the most feared client is the employer who knows just enough about workers' compensation to be a pain in their posterior. Why? It's simple. If you have the knowledge and vocabulary familiar to the adjuster, you can hold them accountable to deliver what is expected of them. This is the essence of cost containment.

An adjuster is responsible for working the phones, maintaining a diary of their existing claims and acting on incoming mail on a daily basis. Phone, Mail and Diary. This is the Trinity of Workers' Compensation claims handling. To forsake that trinity is the beginning of a nightmare for the clientele involved with that particular adjuster. To lose control over a claims diary is an opening for opportunistic elements to create costly litigation and lengthy claims. We say, become proactive. Make a concerted effort to help the adjuster and motivate him/her to provide top-notch customer service to your company as the insurance carrier has promised when they accepted your signed application for insurance and premium. The adjuster will be defensive and resist initially, but your continued efforts will create a productive and effective working relationship.

In the process of your initial contact, get confirmation that the adjuster has sent all statutory letters and made all possible contacts to properly investigate a claim. Hold him and his supervisor accountable for both good and bad results. Keep in mind, however, that an adjuster has at least one diary for each of their own claims. In order for the adjuster to see each claim in his or her inventory, which can range from 150 to 200 claims and occasionally more, they would have to review at least five to twelve files a day or one to three files every hour. Unfortunately, this is not a realistic feat. This effort does not include handling phones, mail, meetings, socializing and any number of other interruptions. Your challenge is to give your claims priority over the duties just described. If you are counting on support from his supervisor, please keep in mind, the supervisor has a diary as well as the adjusters. The only difference is that the supervisor has a diary for each and every claim under their supervision (up to 1500 claims therefore, at least 1500 diaries that must be seen within an acceptable timeframe). Realistically, expect the adjuster to see each file on diary anywhere from 60 to 90 days. That means you need to get familiar with your adjuster very quickly.

Another proactive step employers can to take is to contact the legal defense team and introduce themselves and offer to share as much information as possible with the attorney and create a solid working rapport. It makes a tremendous difference in the level of commitment and effort expended by the attorney. If you are contesting a claim in its entirety, ask the attorney what evidence is needed to succeed.

Here are a few more proactive steps you can take:

1. Gather names of witnesses

2. Gather evidence and send to insurance carrier and attorney

3. Contact the adjuster just prior to various statutory deadlines and court proceedings

4. Attend scheduled depositions and hearings

5. Perform a yearly workplace assessment to better assess your propensity for future claims

6. Implement an employer level claim system

7. Create and enhance your Employee Health and Safety Program

Step 2

Control your X-Mod

With California Workers' Compensation Rates reaching new heights, employers are scrutinizing the calculation of their experience modification factor now, more than ever. Your current workers' compensation premium is closely tied to the experience modification factor calculated by your service providers. Although there is traditionally very little questioning by the employer in the calculation process, an inflated insurance premium will surely result when improper and/or erroneous claims data and payroll information is utilized. By making yourself familiar with the general concept of experience rating you may allocate more concern and attention to the process through which your future workers' compensation premiums are calculated

An Experience Modification factor is like a temperature reading. This tells the employer and everyone else in the Workers' Compensation Insurance Market, if you are, in a sense, running a fever. The strongest employer with a 76 X-mod is paying 24% below the manual rates. (We know few, if any, employers with this X-mod rating, but we'd like to meet more.) This modifier when applied to your manual insurance rate will either raise your premium or maintain them level.

We know that experience rating tailors the cost of insurance to the performance of the individual employer. The higher your experience modifier, the more you are paying in insurance premium when compared to another company in your industry blessed with a lower experience modifier. "Company A" has an X-Mod of 179. "Company B" has an X-Mod of 82. Company A is paying a 79% surcharge over and above their manual rates. Conversely, Company B will be paying 18% below manual rates. Manual premium is the class rate multiplied by your payroll in hundreds of dollars. It is then adjusted by the X-Mod as a percentage. For illustration purposes, a risk that produces a manual premium of $100,000 would then have their respective X-Mod applied. In the case of Company A, they would pay $179,000 ($100,000 x 1.79). On the other side, Company B would pay $82,000 ($100,000 x .82), a difference of $97,000 in premium.

I know it's very confusing, but keep in mind, the original intention of experience rating was to allow the employer to control insurance costs through measurable loss control programs. Given this information, the insurance underwriter, is then asked that crucial question, "is this risk acceptable?" Each underwriter and each insurance company has its own criteria with which to assess this risk. They, theoretically, will take notice of a solid safety and loss control program implemented and stringently pursued and it's the responsibility of your broker to convey to the insurance carrier and prove your risk management efforts so they can take a chance on your losses not breaking their bank.

Loss control and safety programs have proven over the last several years to have a direct impact on loss frequency though, which affect claims losses.

However, your program should be ever changing. Assess and re-assess your company's workers compensation program. Make alterations and corrections in the way you deal with employees. In order to maintain a good exposure record, your "presence" is required on the premises and out in the field. This includes evaluating your employee climate; taking notice of personal relationships developing on your front lines and moreover creating a risk management policy that all employees within your company can understand.

Your broker should be gathering an array of data come Unit Statistical time. Unit-Statistical filing with the State is done six (6) months after the expiration of your first policy (or 18 months after the inception of the same policy) and annually thereafter. Your broker will submit your losses to the WCIRB (Workers' Compensation Insurance Rating Bureau) at Unit Statistical time. They will accumulate all appropriate data including payroll, loss data, class codes, recoveries, credits, etc. Typically, your broker collects crude accounting of your payroll in an attempt to get a head start on the X-Mod calculation process. They are to conduct a final "audit" of your payroll and gather any last minute data.

Today, employers are educating themselves in order to protect their interests and play a more influential role in the calculation of their X-Mod. In order to do this, you will need to know the common errors made in calculating your X-Mod.

- **Payroll Amount is Wrong**

  This error occurs when initial payroll total rather than audited final payroll total, is reported for one or more job classifications. If the amount of payroll reported is less than the actual payroll, your X-Mod will be inflated.

- **The Report Contains Claims That Should Be Charged To Another Employer**

  This is common when different employers share similar names. For example, ABC Company can be confused with "A Bee See Company."

- **Claims Costs Were Improperly Stated**

  This occurs from simple clerical errors in transposition, deletion or exclusion while transferring statistical information on to the Unit Stat Report.

- **Losses May Be Valued as of an Incorrect Valuation Date**

  Claim costs shown on the unit stat report should match precisely with those shown on the insurer's loss runs as of the proper valuation date used for unit stat report purposes. If the terminal date for the rating period is March 31, the loss run utilized should be valued as of March 31 as well.

- **Changes in claim status, which occurred prior to preparation of the unit stat report might not be accurately reflected in the report**

  Last minute efforts by service providers to reduce outstanding reserve amounts may fail. In turn, these vital changes in claim totals will not be reflected on the loss runs used to prepare the unit stat report. This will inevitably reflect a much higher value being reported to the rating bureau for those particular claims, resulting in an inflated X-Mod.

- **Credit was not given for subrogation recoveries**
  Subrogation recoveries are usually obtained months or even years after the cost of a claim has been reported to the bureau. To compensate for this occurrence, some states, such as California, provide for a recalculation of the X-Mod.

Verifying the accuracy of your X-Mod is not only wise, it's smart business and should be standard practice especially where there has been a sharp increase in the X-Mod and resulting premium.

To protect yourself, you should:

- Obtain the most recent unit statistical report from your agent, broker or insurer.

- Compare reported payroll amounts shown for each job classification to the audited payroll amounts to make sure they are identical.

- Check the claims listed on your unit statistical report with the claims appearing on your loss run. Are they all yours? Are the claim totals correct?

- Make sure the status of each claim is true and correct. In other words, are there any claims listed as open that are or have recently been closed?

- Make yourself keenly aware of the current status of your claims. This is paramount in determining errors on insurers' loss runs. Question everything. Do not interpret what is provided to you to be the final word.

- Monitoring the status of all open claims ensures that the claims are being adjusted in the most cost-effective manner.

- Develop and nourish a relationship with the claims adjuster charged to handle your claims. In a thankless industry, civility can go a very long way with the adjuster. An adjuster will take the time to call you back when they feel comfortable speaking with you.

- By keeping your finger on the pulse of your claims and opening the door to frequent conversations with your adjusting team, you will be better able to affect positive change in your loss history. Let them know you are there to help in reducing overall claim costs.

The effects of an erroneous X-Mod are detrimental and can last for up to three years or more. If you have experienced a sharp increase in your X-Mod, you should immediately take steps to identify, verify and correct the data on which the X-Mod is based. By erring on the side of caution, this will make you familiar with the underlying basic concepts of experience rating calculations. You will not only feel confident in your X-Mod, you will sleep better knowing the shop is being kept.

Loss Control — Controlling what you can control

Unfortunately, as an employer, you are at the mercy of many forces. One of those forces is your agent/broker. If what he or she is selling you sounds too good to be true, it probably is. Although most brokers are sincere, be realistic with their promises and take them all with a grain of salt, because in reality what you can control is merely an image and it's called your "presence".

You run a tight ship from the pre-employment screening and physicals to the Monday morning tailgate safety meetings in the yard at 5:30 a.m. This is how you control your losses; by allowing your "presence" to seen, heard and felt at the worksite. If this is part of your safety and loss control program, as much as you think it's not working, it is. As we mentioned earlier, a risk management policy should be so simple and easy to understand that employees of all levels can easily understand it. The reason for this is that it communicates your risk management goals and purpose to all under your employ. The "purpose", is that you are actively committed to the safety and welfare of your employees. Safety meetings support your commitment and get employees to buy in to it if done right. Constant coaching of front line supervisors commits them to the company's safety goals and maintains your risk management philosophy fresh in your employee's minds. What else is there to worry about besides your occupational class code which is out of your control; past loss history, which you can't change and is out of your control and manual premium rates; still, out of your control.

Concentrate on those things that are directly within your control. If you are the slightest bit unhappy or uncomfortable with your agent/broker's past performance or service, start shopping around. Find an agent/broker you feel comfortable with and that is willing to commit to your program as well. What else are they bringing to the table besides the "best deal"?

Evaluate and re-evaluate your relationship with your current industrial clinic. There are a lot of industrial clinics willing to go the extra mile for your business. Contracts are the catalysts for complacency. Foster competition by shopping for service providers.

Step 3

Creating a Proactive Team

As an employer, when it comes to workers compensation and risk management programs, you have two options: the reactive approach or the proactive approach. Surprisingly the majority of employers choose the reactive approach.

A reactive approach, however, places your company in a vulnerable position, especially if your risk management model is weak or non-existent. A reactive approach literally places the success of your workers comp program in the hands of an adjuster *after* an injury occurs, which is too little too late. We choose the proactive approach.

Proactive approaches involve analysis of your present incident procedures or lack thereof; establishing goals and desired outcomes for your program; creating procedures and protocols that are consistent with the company business philosophy; creating a risk management policy that every employee in the company can clearly understand and follow and more. Sounds like a lot of work, right? Well, it is.

Developing your Workers' Compensation Team

Although larger corporate employers have specialized human resource departments, many departments handle a myriad of responsibilities including Workers' Compensation matters.

Occasionally employers create a workers compensation coordinator position to help begin the claims process and affect more attentive file handling from an insurance carrier. However, if your loss experience is minimal, you may not need a workers compensation coordinator to control, maintain, mitigate, organize and make some kind of sense out of issues dealing with workers' compensation. If your company maintains high-risk occupations and a fairly consistent frequency of injuries, then keeping a coordinator on staff may be a very good idea. Workers' Compensation is a weak link all by itself. By adding this task to your Human Resource department will likely create weaker links within the company. But this chapter is not about creating a workers compensation coordinator position within your organization, but rather it is about creating a team of people within your organization who can create and implement a procedure for recognizing potential hazards, affecting solutions to those hazards, train the workforce to recognize and eliminate those hazards from the workplace. Should an incident occur on the worksite, your team, much like a fire department, will use a systematic approach to confirm, report and follow up on the progress of the claims as they occur.

This is the proactive approach that will save your company thousands of dollars!

The importance of effective team building cannot be overlooked at this point. In order for your program to run efficiently, it is crucial to match the appropriate personalities to the right duties.

The first step to team building is deciding who will lead the team. Who will make the important decisions? Will you hire a safety professional to head the team? Or will you assign the task to an internal department head in the company. If your company is a small or emerging business, this decision will be obvious; however your challenges may be greater.

Another team member you may wish to consider is a safety team leader. This person would be charged with coordinating regular safety meetings for all employees. Another aspect of their duties would include safety walk-through and worksite safety reviews.

One person should be designated as the "go to" person with all matters related to Workers' Compensation and appointed by management. This way, there is never a question as to authority. There will never be a question as to what the company's management's plan is to handle these matters. Your coordinator should report directly to, and only to, management. All others should report to your Workers' Compensation Coordinator. This person should be delegating all tasks required of other supervisory personnel (inside and outside); should have current job descriptions meeting strict ADA (American's with Disabilities Act) Guidelines. For more information on Americans with Disabilities act, visit ADA Home Page at http://ada.gov/. In general, today's job descriptions must take into account and list specifically the duties required of the position in question. A job description should elaborate on time required to complete certain tasks; must include frequency and detailed weight specifications. For example, the job description must outline the fact that 20% of the day (1.6 hours) is spent refilling the parts hopper with cases of aluminum weighing 3 pounds, 8 pounds and 16 pounds (depending on the size and type of product in question).

Along with current job descriptions of all positions, a separate description should be attached for a modified position. This will address a speedy return to work. Again, this is all of the pre-planning phase to ready your company in case an injury occurs. Each and every position should have at least one (maybe two or three) modified positions outlined in the same vein as the original job descriptions were devised. Each modified job description will be tailor made to the position for which your employee was injured.

Not only will your level of preparedness make the process of filing the claim with your claims administration office easier, it will make a difference to underwriters considering your company's risk. This level of preparedness will make the job of the underwriter a little easier when they can see you have an ironclad plan in place should an injury take place. This can directly affect your annual premium.

What to expect once the injury occurs

Despite the best lost-control program, injuries WILL occur. This is unavoidable unless you choose to close your doors. For most business owners, risk-avoidance is not an option however; risk-reduction is something we all partake in daily. For the most part, we choose to transfer the risk to insurance companies in the form of a workers' compensation insurance policy. For a "reduced fee" (premium) you are guaranteed against the uncertainty of a large loss. That's the extent of workers' compensation insurance. Once an injury occurs, knowing what to do next is critical.

When a five-alarm fire rings in the firehouse, a plan is in place like no other in existence. Firefighting pros know exactly what their role as they prepare to head out to a fire. Time is of the essence in this example and they know that every second counts. The same zeal should be placed on your Workers' Compensation program. There should be no guesswork when it comes to your reaction to an industrial injury.

For an industrial injury to be "industrial" it must meet the AOE-COE test. AOE/COE refers to an industrial accident's qualifying criteria. "Arising Out of Employment" and occurring in the "Course of Employment" is a nice way of saying that the injury must have taken place while the worker was completing a task for which he/she was hired. If you split this AOE-COE test up, it's not an industrial injury — that simple. There are many instances of injuries satisfying one or the other half of the AOE-COE test. For the most part, the "Course of Employment" is easier to disprove. An example is a salesman on a sales call paying a visit to the Horse Track to make a quick bet. He trips and falls while walking from the establishment to his car. In this case, he has clearly deviated from the activities for which he receives compensation from his employer. An example of not meeting the AOE (Arising Out of Employment) is where a bartender decides to try her skills as a deep-fry Cook and burns her arm with scalding oil. This injury was in the Course Of Employment as she was at work when this happened however; the injury did not arise from duties required of her while bartending (unless the employer instructed the employee to try the new duties).

If you do not have an established workers comp or risk management program in place, it is best that you notify your claims administration office when an injury occurs and let them instruct you how to handle each unique situation. (However, in such a case you forgo a proactive approach for one of more passive participation.) The employee, witness or authorized personnel must inform you that an injury took place at work in order for you to advise the injured worker to seek medical attention. Make it your policy to mandate a visit to your industrial medical clinic despite not desiring immediate medical care.

Employer knowledge is said to have existed when any one in a supervisory position has been placed on notice of the allegation of an industrial injury, specific or cumulative in nature. In California, the Employer's First Report of Industrial Injury is to be completed and sent to the claims agency along with any other supporting documentation you feel will help in the investigation of this allegation. The Employee's Claim

Form Workers Compensation Benefits (form DWC-1) must be provided to the employee within 24 hours.

Once you have been made aware of the work injury, the clock starts ticking for ALL parties. Some of the first things we look for when initiating a full AOE-COE investigation in the compensability of a Workers' Compensation claim, is supporting documentation from co-workers and immediate supervisors. There are many occasions, more often than not, when front line supervisors fail to notify management of an allegation or incident of injury. Yet the front-line supervisor was told about this injury 3 weeks prior and they are just now telling you. The date of knowledge will have occurred 3 weeks ago and not when that supervisor reported the incident to you. Your claims handlers will only have one week to maintain medical control and just over 60 days to complete their investigation. This may not seem to be a big deal in the case where the injury is clear and there is no question as to the legitimacy of the allegations however, it's when the injury is highly suspect that precious time has been wasted due to the fact there was no plan in place when the incident occurs.

Bottom line: Be prepared. Make sure your front line managers and supervisors know exactly what is expected of them. Be confident that they are well trained in asking the right questions and that they know your company's policies regarding industrial injuries. In the case of on-site projects (plumbing, framing, soil-testing, etc.) some employers adopt the philosophy mandating supervisors to carry claim forms and job descriptions unique to their employee's occupation in case an industrial injury occurs. Employers will designate a medical facility within close proximity to the work site in case a work injury occurs.

Step 4

Creating Meaningful Alternative Employment

Ideally, returning injured workers back to gainful employment is the goal of workers' compensation, right? However, we cannot get them back to the exact point in time prior to the injury occurring but, getting them as close to pre-injury status is attainable and any self-respecting claims professional seeks to achieve this. If we cannot, we must compensate these individuals for their loss to compete in the open labor market.

There are many time-sensitive activities the adjusting team must contend with and there are a myriad of time windows within which to complete such tasks. For example, California employers who do not have an approved Medical Provider Network, you, the employer, have only thirty (30) days of medical control from when you are made reasonably knowledgeable an industrial injury occurred. The adjuster must accept or delay a claim within fourteen (14) days of the date of knowledge. The adjuster has ninety (90) days within which to decide the compensability of a claim.

In some states there is a three-day waiting period before an injured worker will be paid temporary disability. There are two general exceptions to this rule: (1) If the injured worker is hospitalized, or (2) if the employee is disabled for more than 21 days. Thus, by having a return to work plan in place, thousands of dollars per lost time claim will be retained.

As we suggested in earlier chapters, the creation of meaningful, ADA compliant, job descriptions for every position in your company is a good step. Ease of access to these job descriptions is key. The job description will allow the treating doctor to make a return to work determination. Having a job description for a pre-determined temporary modified position will make the doctor's decision for clear wording on return to work, even easier. You will have, in your hand, a medical statement indicating your employee, injured while cutting blue widgets may return to work beginning tomorrow sanding yellow widgets. You have just taken every excuse away from the injured worker.

Keep in mind this is a temporary modified position or "transitional" position. All parties expect the work restrictions to lessen over time while the injured workers' capacity and tolerance increase. The transitional position should change with increased ability and should not last for more than six months. If the position lasts longer than six months you run the risk of a discrimination suit should the employee be terminated when he is unable to return to his usual and customary occupation. The longer you maintain the same modified position, the more valid their argument for "discrimination" will be when you tell the adjuster that you have no permanent modified position available for the employee.

The tasks for a transitional position must increase as the injured workers' ability to take on more physical activity increase. An example of when employers get into some trouble occurs when the same temporary modified position is provided for six months or longer. Should the treating doctor declare the injured workers' medical condition to be permanent & stationary (not getting any better and not getting any worse—plateau), and the employee is unable to return to his original occupation, the insurance adjuster will send a form titled "Notice of Offer of Modified or Alternate Work". (The introduction of vocational rehabilitation varies from state to state.) This form is asking if you have a permanent modified position for this injured worker. Should you answer, "no", to the question of availability of such work, yet you provided a temporary modified position for a long enough period, this can be construed as having permanent modified available thus necessitating the filing of a wrongful termination claim if the employee is terminated or referred to a vocational rehabilitation plan.

Having an injured worker back to work can sometimes make you feel like a hostage in your own company. Injured workers are to be treating no differently than the other employees however, we know better. It's rare to come across an injured worker these days who is simply grateful for the opportunity to work after sustaining an industrial injury. Unfortunately, you will always have your share of injured workers who maintain an attitude of "entitlement".

In today's litigious society employers tend to feel as if they are walking on eggshells when dealing with injured employees. It is important to maintain a strict personnel policy overall and clarify to staff that all employees are to be treated according to company policy no matter what their injury status. Discuss hiring and firing processes with labor counsel in order to establish concrete policy. Then communicate this policy to the entire workforce regularly.

Firing an injured worker for cause is always a touchy subject. In such cases it is vital that ongoing history and documentation of the employee's behaviors be maintained. It is likely that termination of an injured employee will be upheld if documentation and history supports the termination. However, failure to logically and legitimately support an employee's termination could put an employer on the losing end of a discrimination and wrongful termination suit. So beware and always consult with labor counsel when considering termination of an injured employee.

Step 5

Have an Effective Return to Work Program

Your program is coming together! You've taken proactive steps to understand your X-mod, making your presence known to both employees and your insurance carrier or third party administrator. Well, here's where it starts to come together. Here's where the real money savings begin! You're going to bring your employee back to work.

In the previous step you created alternative and meaningful work in anticipation of a work related injury that resulted in lost time from work. The implementation of that plan and the cooperation of the doctor create a powerful element in your program …the Return to Work program.

An effective Return to Work program requires cooperation from everyone involved; the employer, employee and the doctor. However the primary point of an effective Return to Work is to get the employee back to work within the 30 day Employer Medical Control Period. Doing so greatly reduces the probability of litigation, ensures the probability of the employee returning to permanent work and greatly reduces claims costs by minimizing temporary disability benefits and eliminating the need for vocational rehabilitation benefits. Bottom line that means reduced claim losses, which equals lower X-mod, which means money in your pocket – savings!

In order to get started, written job descriptions of every occupation in your company must be obtained. It is recommended that State job description forms be used. Most state approved job description forms include specific aspects of an occupation including weights and measures used in executing a particular occupation as well as the frequency of various physical demands of an occupation. The State Job Description form, likewise, is recognized by the major bureaucratic departments such as OSHA, Workers Compensation Appeals Board and Rehabilitation Unit. When an injury does occur on the jobsite, this form will be provided to the doctor by the employee. The doctor will also prescribe the physical limitations as they pertain to the employee's job. It is likely at that point, that the employee will be placed on temporary disability based on that one job description. However, being the *proactive* employer that you are; you have also anticipated this moment and also created job description forms outlining modified versions of the employee's job. This form will also accompany the claimant to the doctor's office and unless the claimant is severely injured or incapacitated, the doctor will likely release the claimant back to work to the modified position.

The job description form will also be utilized by the physical therapist as a reference as he begins to work with the injured employee. It will provide medical objectives for the therapist during work hardening, which translates to reduced medical and therapy costs!

In order to ensure an effective outcome of the Return to Work process, you, the employer must be prepared sell the modified work program to the doctor, but more importantly this aspect of the claim requires the employer's presence. By monitoring the progress of the employee and the doctor during the modified work period, especially during the crucial 30-day employer controlled medical timeframe, the likelihood of a successful return to full duty can be realized. This sends a powerful message to the rest of the workforce. The purpose of all of this is to maintain medical control and reduce losses due to disability. However, in some states such as California, if the employer has an approved Medical Provider Network, they will maintain medical control for the life of the claim and the main focus of your efforts will be with returning the employee to work.

Modified vs. Alternative Work

So, you're sitting there saying "What's the difference between Modified and Alternative work!" Yes, we know it can get confusing. However, both can and do save you money only at different times.

Modified work is implemented soon after the initial date of injury. It is the employer's and employee's opportunity to forgo time off work and temporary disability benefits. The incentive for the employee to participate is that he will continue to receive a full salary during his recuperation on the modified work schedule rather than receive only a portion of his salary through temporary disability benefits. Modified work simultaneously reassures the employee that he will maintain his position with the company and that the employer has a viable interest in the employee's return to full duty. It's a win-win situation.

Alternative work relates directly to Vocational Rehabilitation. It refers to a new and different position within the employer's company where the employee can return to work and perform his duties within any permanent restrictions prescribed by the doctor. When an injury does create a situation so as to prevent the employee from returning to his or her usual and customary job, the employee becomes eligible to receive vocational rehabilitation benefits, which include vocational retraining. (Please note that it is feasible that the employee remain in a modified position up to this point) At this juncture the decision to retrain the employee in a new occupation is left to the doctor. The creation of an alternative occupation with the employer would enable the employee to remain with the employer and at a pay rate similar to that of the original position. In contrast, vocational retraining into a new occupation usually leads to an entry -level position with entry-level wages. Successful placement in a new occupation is slim. Retrained employees, more often than not, fail to secure positions in their new vocational venture. It's a disillusioning fact of the system and as a result states such as California have begun a phase out of the benefit. Nevertheless, pre-determined alternative work or an employer's willingness to provide it reduces the cost of a workers compensation claim considerably.

Notes:

Step 6

Maintain a Presence

It's challenging enough managing the ins and outs of business on a daily basis, but now I have to add something else to the list. Maintain a presence in the workplace. If you take that literally, you can imagine an armed guard tower watching over your employees as they work on the floor below. Well, you're not that far off. The only difference is that it needs to be done on a psychological level. Although it sounds condescending, as employers you must concede, employees can sometimes behave like children. In this case the children have endless resources guiding them, if not egging them on, to litigate their claims. However, likewise they recognize the control of authority in the workplace.

You didn't ask to be involved, but now that you are... Creating a presence in the workplace begins before an injury is reported. It begins with the creation of proactive safety policies and procedures also known as Injury Illness and Prevention (IIP) or Emergency Health and Safety programs (EHS); procedures that are communicated to the employee and practiced by the employer's workers comp team. The practice and rehearsal of the plan is a signal to the workforce. The employer is in control. This is a presence.

Once an injury is reported, the clock begins to tick. Under California workers compensation rules, if there is no Medical Provider Network, the employer has only a 30-day medical control over the employee. It is imperative that the employees participate in the employer's workers compensation program from the very first day. The employee must know the expectations of the employer and must be coached to meet those expectations from the moment an injury alleged. The mere allegation of an industrial injury is all that it takes to set your workers compensation team into action and the employee must be made aware of this, both overtly and subtly. A well thought out Emergency, Health & Safety (EHS) plan is a great way to develop a presence in the workplace. The more employees take note of their employer's involvement, the more they begin to buy into the entire company safety effort.

How do I maintain a presence in the workplace? Good question. Here's the plan:

* Designate a Workers' Compensation Coordinator. All aspects of workers compensation are handled by this individual, from communicating the employer's expectations to the workforce to driving an injured employee to the clinic. The candidate for this position should be someone with workers compensation claims background; have exceptional leadership qualities; have excellent communication abilities and more importantly be empathetic and compassionate. Should you be fortunate enough to find such a candidate ... pay them generously. Their expertise will save you hundreds of thousands of dollars!

- Set a standard. Communicate your expectations of each and every employee before an injury occurs. Weekly safety meetings should reiterate the process for reporting a claim to the employer and as to when medical status and updates are to be reported.

- Maintain contact with injured worker, adjuster & defense attorney (if the claim litigates). Request that the insurance carrier assign a particular claims adjuster to your account and then make it a point to contact that adjuster every time the claim reaches a statutory milestone in order to ensure that notices have been issued on a timely basis.

- Document and archive job descriptions for existing positions, modified positions and alternative work within your company. Send employee to industrial clinic with job description making clear Return to Work intentions and the ready availability of modified work. Most doctors will comply unless the employee has sustained a traumatic injury.

- Learn the right questions to ask of an adjuster; of an employee and of the doctor. By doing this you make all parties accountable for their roles in the life of a workers compensation claim. The results of this proactive approach, is a drastic reduction of penalties and timely action throughout the claim, which translates to huge savings!

By the time you are done, every party involved in a claim should know who you are, what you do and more importantly, what you expect from them! Settle for nothing less.

Step 7

Manage Your Injured Workers

No one can say with absolute certainty that your employees will not litigate their workers compensation claim. And we must admit that there are many occasions when an employee should consider legal representation. However, many times an employee litigates his claim because outside forces have gotten to him first. And unfortunately those outside forces promise great wealth and an opportunity to stick it to the employer.

A big part of a workers compensation coordinator's job is to assume the empathetic role of employee caretaker. The first contact with the employee should be the coordinator, who takes the time to explain to the employee what they can expect as the workers compensation process moves forward. More importantly is to ensure the employee that they still have a job and that everything will be done to ensure that. The point being, if an injured employee knows what to expect next, they are less likely to litigate.

Keeping Track of Injured Workers

It's hard enough remembering everyone's name let alone their claim status. Maintain documentation related to each employee's workers compensation claim by creating a file outlining the progress of the injured worker's case. Review the file regularly every 30 to sixty days and contact the claim adjuster for an update. This will allow you to keep track of all parties involved on your behalf and will keep them accountable should you ever have to back track. Here are some more tips to help you track your injured worker's progress.

- Follow everything up with a letter. If it seems important, send the letter certified/return receipt

- Make sure that the employee calls after each and every doctors' visit if he or she is medically unable to return to the jobsite

- Report any and all changes in condition or employment status to the insurance carrier

- Make sure follow up visits and/or physical therapy sessions are scheduled during off hours when at all possible. Most occupational clinics such as a 24/7 industrial clinics can accommodate most schedules.

An Employer' Role in A Litigated Claim

Well, here we go again. Another litigated workers comp case. You were sitting there minding your own business, looking through the day's mail when you come across an envelope from a law office. We know the rest of the story. You see inside that envelope is the start of a long and drawn out statutory process. One that weighs heavily on the fact that the burden of proof lies wholly with the employer, which in turn gives rise to a long list of abuses. Unfortunately, insurance carriers are not necessarily in the business of providing counseling or coaching services to employers when their claims litigate due to the sheer number of litigated claims they receive monthly.

In California, the first thing to come across your desk is a Letter of Representation, an Employee Claim Form and an Application for Adjudication of Claim. If these documents are received on an ongoing claim, it is basically the employee appealing the level of benefits being administered with the belief that he is entitled to more (technically speaking). In reality, employees seldom know why they have retained an attorney, other that the fact that they want more money out of the claim. Nevertheless, now's a good time to start keeping a file on your claimant if you haven't already started!

Do you recall we said that an employer's presence needs to be made in the workplace? Good. Because your presence is now required at the Workers Compensation Appeals Board. That's right. Without your involvement in the litigation process there will be only one side to be heard. Along with that, it is in this aspect of a workers compensation claim that the employer stands to incur many of the losses that cause an experience mod to go up.

You'd be surprised how influential an employer's presence can be through the life of a litigated claim. Throughout the litigation process there needs to be a constant. Claim adjusters come and go quite frequently. Each has his, or her, own level of expertise, experience, poise and commitment to the fiduciary responsibility to the insured. The same can be said for the defense attorney hired by the insurance carrier. So that pretty much leaves you – the employer. Your presence and the presence of witnesses at the major activities in the workers compensation process serve a major purpose. It keeps an employee honest, or at least as honest as can be expected. It also serves to bring about a more concerted effort from the defense attorney. It's the difference between going in with the purpose to settle a claim versus going in to defend the insured. It is imperative that you understand that in statutory compensatory system, the burden of proof for any claim, at least in California, lies with the employer and it is much more cost effective for the carrier to "settle" a claim rather than defend it. There is no right or wrong per the labor code, so that means winning can cost a lot of money. Our purpose is to prevent employees from litigating by creating a proactive presence in the workplace, which along with effective risk management practices can make for an affordable workers comp premium. So here are some practices to follow when you have a litigated claim:

- Follow up with claims examiner to confirm that they have referred the file to a defense attorney – although there are qualified examiners out there, very few have mastered the rules of practice and procedures. Coupled with the already backlogged work, an examiner has little time to actually perform many of the necessary duties required to keep a litigated claim current. If they are not going to refer the file to an attorney from the onset, find out what the adjuster's defense strategy is going to be.

- Utilize a small attorney firm- by doing this it allows both the claims adjuster and the employer easier access to the attorney and allows both the greater ability to take part in the litigation strategy.

- Meet your defense team – Call the defense team and get to know the attorney that will be handling the claim. Ask questions such as "What kind of evidence would you like to see?" "Will there be a deposition?"

- Be present at the deposition- Many times you may not be allowed into the proceedings, however, your presence and the employee's knowledge of your presence could have a significant psychological effect and prevent the employee from exaggerating his position.

- Attend the Mandatory Settlement Conferences and trials. Always remember you are the number one witness. One sided testimony makes for a huge settlement. More often than not, employers do not attend a hearing, which gives the attorneys an opportunity to settle the claim out. At times that is the best solution, but in reality it's an opportunity for the attorney and the claims adjuster to close a file. However, the majority of the time it's the employer who gets the short end of the stick. You can change that.

Step 8

Methods of Settlement —
Search for a Win-Win Solution to End Claims

The time has finally come! Every available resource has been expended and it's now time to settle the claim. Unfortunately even claims that we believe are not compensable are settled. That's the reality of the workers compensation system. So as we get over the pain of it, let's briefly talk about methods of claims settlement.

- Compromise & Release – this is the preferred method of settlement for insurance carriers. This document releases all future rights to compensation for future benefits that the employee may be entitled to including future death benefits. All this in exchange for a lump sum of cash. Settling a claim in this manner can be both good and not so good for the employer. On the one hand, by settling in this manner the employer is off the claim for good. On the other hand the cost of such a settlement can be high and as a result have a negative effect on your ex-mod, which means next years premium could be higher; significantly higher. It is a good idea to discuss claims that are close to settlement with your broker, the underwriter and the adjuster for the purpose of estimating next year's premium. However, by the time a claim is ready to settle in this manner, all options have likely been exhausted.

- Stipulations with Request for Award – for employee's who remain with their employer and whose injury has left them with the need for future medical treatment, this method of settlement will keep the claim open indefinitely. The employee will then continue to treat on an as-needed basis. This method is utilized mainly with employer's who are self-insured and self-administered. The down side of this is that the number of open claims continue to grow, which in turn may drive up the cost of excess insurance. One method of reducing these open claims is by offering to settle the future medical claims of former employees and retirees via Compromise & Release. Insurance carriers will avoid this manner of settlement as it prevents them from closing the claim, which is the primary goal of a claims office.

- Arbitration – A great opportunity to settle a claim in a reasonably fair manner. This is one of the few times that the employer actually has an opportunity to get a fair shake. However, with the legions of applicant attorneys out there, it is unlikely that one of them ay agree to mediation. We'll stop here on this subject.

- Structured Settlement – the only win-win solution in claims settlement is the structured settlement. The beauty of the structured settlement is that it gives both parties what they want. In this type of settlement a structured settlement specialist facilitates the agreement by providing the financial vehicle with which to fund the deal. The employer puts up money (or premium) into an immediate fixed annuity of a guaranteed interest rate, which is provided by the structured settlement specialist. The employee and his attorney get a lump sum of up-front money to cover attorney fees. The money in the annuity will then provide the employee with a fixed monthly payment that is guaranteed to a fixed period of time. The beauty of this deal is that this agreement is wrapped around a Compromise & Release agreement, which means that the employee forfeits his rights to further benefits. The benefit for the insurance carrier or self insured employer is that the amount of money put forth on this settlement is thousands less than the money required to settle via a lump sum settlement. This method of settlement is also very effective in resolving civil and labor related lawsuits.

Get Your Carrier/TPA to Go the Extra Mile

As you can see by now workers compensation claims is a hands-on, proactive coaching experience. What makes it increasingly difficult is the fact that in such a system, the cards are automatically stacked against the employer. But here is what we believe you are entitled to:

- Ask for more than a yearly claims status report – many carriers and third party administrators will advise you of their policy to provide only one yearly claims review per year. Those companies that get more than one review per year are more than likely the larger clients in terms of premium. However, the time to negotiate that kind of service should be at the time you are purchasing the policy or contracting the administrating service.

- Are they asking for Mod/Alt work? – Thousands if not millions of dollars are lost each year by the failure of claims handlers to ask that question, "Is modified or alternative work available?" That's why it is our practice to coach employers to advise the claims handler from the onset that modified work is/is not available. However, as we stated in previous chapters, the existence of modified work can save you thousands of dollars lost per claim, which would have been paid out in temporary disability benefits. So why isn't this question being asked? It could be many things, but from a proactive point of view, "why?" is not an effective question. Rather "how?" and "who?" would be the empowering question to ask. "How can we ensure that the employee will return to modified or alternative work?" and "Who can help us get this worker back to the jobsite?"

One Last Tip

Ask the claims adjuster if they have sent ALL required claim notices – in California claims, as in many states, claims examiners are responsible for sending out the appropriate claim notice on a timely basis. Failure to do so will result in the insurance carrier being fined by the Department of Industrial Relations for failure to provide timely notice to the injured worker. Those fines are paid by the insurance carrier and are quite minimal. And if you recall from earlier chapters the costs of those adjuster errors would be added to the employer's losses and the ex mod would grow as a result. We encourage employers to ask about these notices often.

The Latest Development in Workers Compensation – The Medicare Set Aside (MSA)

In 1965 Congress established the Medicare program to provide medical care for the elderly, disabled and individuals suffering from end stage renal disease. However, after 15 years Medicare took steps to ensure its fiscal integrity. In other words, Medicare found itself paying the bill for thousands of injured workers who had settled their future medical benefits via a Compromise and Release. The same was true of plaintiffs receiving medical benefits through auto and other liability policies. The result was the need for Medicare to assert its secondary payer status in cases where a primary payer was present. In 1980 Congress established the Medicare Secondary Payer Statute ensuring that Medicare would remain the secondary payer if a primary payer was present. Twenty years later, the law actually took effect and claim adjusters and Medicare beneficiaries across America were notified via a memorandum from the Centers for Medicare and Medicaid Services (CMS) that Medicare's interests was to be considered in every case where future medical treatment was to be settled out. CMS provided a formula for future cost projection and a format for complying with this new directive. The method for reporting this information to CMS was through a report termed Medicare Set Aside. The first line of insurance to be tested was workers compensation and once the program was streamlined, other lines of insurance would have to follow suit.

In a nutshell CMS has stated future medical costs need to be set aside in an interest bearing account so that the injured worker can pay for his own future treatment for the injured body part. Medicare would remain the secondary payer once the future medical treatment funds are permanently depleted.

This directive and subsequent ones which have followed has caused an increase in settlement amounts as well as the speed with which a claim can be settled. The affect on the employer is that it will cause claims to remain open longer as well as cause an increase in expenditures in the handling of the claims.

It is to the employer's benefit to keep their employees working and create transitional employment in the workplace. It is also important to ensure that Medicare's interests are being considered in every claim that is settling future medical care as failure to do so will leave the employer exposed to potential conditional payment claims from CMS. As discussed previously, request a quarterly claim review and make it a point to query the adjuster about the need for a Medicare Set Aside in each case that is being considered for settlement via Compromise and Release or where future medical costs are being settled out. Should you have open cases with your claims administrator, it is important to know if the employee is Medicare eligible or close to it. The identification of a case requiring a Medicare Set Aside can increase the cost of settlement by thousands of dollars. It is important that you get a better understanding of this statute from your claims administrator. Keep in mind, this is a federal statute and nationwide all employers, third party administrators, insurance carriers and self insured employers are required to conform to the requirements as laid out by the Centers for Medicare and Medicaid Services (CMS).

Final

Well those are the 8 Steps. Twenty-five years of workers comp experience has allowed us to bring to you the most effective actions that could bring about a decrease in your premium. It's all very un-scientific, but very psychological. The point is getting people to act on your behalf; getting your employees involved in the effort to reduce injuries on the job; holding those involved in your claims accountable for their actions or inactions and raising the bar on your expectations. Believe it or not, the majority of participants in your claims will rise to the occasion.

Workers Compensation all over America is changing, however insurance carriers and third party administrators have in the past failed to change with it. Insurance carriers and third party administrators continue to operate using administration models of 30 years ago. We believe that it affects employers directly. While we cannot absolutely guarantee that these methods will change your economic situation, we do believe it will give you control over this growing problem. In the future, look for the emergence of self-insured groups in your state as employers devise new ways to alleviate their workers compensation issues. In California, this has already become a reality. But overall, we recommend employers remain closely involved in their risk management programs and closely manage the parties they have entrusted with the welfare of their workers. And most importantly, remember, risk management is in reality simple communication; just a sincere effort to get your employees on board and believing in what you are trying to accomplish on their behalf … a safe workplace.

Appendix

Links & Resources

Guidebook for Injured Workers

www.dir.ca.gov/CHSWC/CHSWCworkercompguidebook.pdf

CAL OSHA

http://www.californiaosha.info

Division of Occupational Safety & Health

http://www.dir.ca.gov/DOSH/

Department of Industrial Relations Home page

http://www.dir.ca.gov/

CA Employers Guide to Workers Compensation in CA – 60 page guidebook

http://www.dir.ca.gov/DWC/erguide.pdf

DWC California Labor Code

http://www.leginfo.ca.gov/cgi-
bin/calawquery?codesection=lab&codebody=

Industrial Medical Council -Evaluation Procedures

http://www.dir.ca.gov/t8/ch1a4.html

Industrial Medical Council -Evaluation Procedures – Minimum Time requirements

http://www.dir.ca.gov/t8/ch1a4_5.html

Industrial Medical Council - Practice Parameters for the Treatment of Common Industrial Injuries

http://www.dir.ca.gov/t8/ch1a7.html

Department of Industrial Relations - Division of Labor Statistics and Research

Occupational Injury or Illness Reports and Records

http://www.dir.ca.gov/t8/ch7sb1.html

Title 8 Medical Regs & Regulations

http://www.dir.ca.gov/t8/ch4_5sb1a5.html

The Occupational Safety and Health Administration

http://www.osha.gov/SLTC/smallbusiness/chklist.html#safety

Additional Resources

Workers Comp Appeals Board Addresses

CA WCAB MAILING ADDRESS

P. O Box 429459

San Francisco, CA 94142-9459

WCAB District Offices

Anaheim

Workers' Compensation Appeals Board

1661 N. Raymond Avenue Ste 200
Anaheim, CA 92801-1162

Bakersfield

Workers' Compensation Appeals Board

1800 30th Street, Rm 100
Bakersfield, CA 93301-1929

Eureka

Workers' Compensation Appeals Board

100 "H" Street Rm. 202
Eureka, CA 95501-0481

Fresno

Workers' Compensation Appeals Board

2550 Mariposa Street, Rm. 4078
Fresno, CA 93721-2280

Goleta

Workers' Compensation Appeals Board

6755 Holister Ave Suite 100
Goleta, CA 93117-3018

Grover Beach

Workers' Compensation Appeals Board

1562 Grand Avenue
Grover Beach, CA 93433-2261

Long Beach

Workers' Compensation Appeals Board

300 Oceangate Drive, Suite 200
Long Beach, CA 90802-4339

Los Angeles

Workers' Compensation Appeals Board

320 West 4th Street, 9th Floor
Los Angeles, CA 90013-1105

Oakland

Workers' Compensation Appeals Board

1515 Clay Street, 6th Floor
Oakland, CA 94612-1402

Oxnard

Workers' Compensation Appeals Board

2220 East Gonzales Road, Suite 100
Oxnard, CA 93030

Pomona

Workers' Compensation Appeals Board

732 Corporate Center Drive
Pomona, CA 91768-1601

Riverside

Workers' Compensation Appeals Board

3737 Main Street, Ste 300
Riverside, CA 92501-3337

Salinas

Workers' Compensation Appeals Board

1880 North Main Street, 1st Floor
Salinas, CA 93906-2016

San Diego

Workers' Compensation Appeals Board

7575 Metropolitan Road, Suite 202
San Diego, CA 92102-4402

San Jose

Workers' Compensation Appeals Board

100 Paseo de San Antonio, Suite 241
San Jose, CA 95113-1482

Santa Monica

Workers' Compensation Appeals Board

2701 Ocean Park Blvd. Ste 220
Santa Monica, CA 90405-5212

Stockton

Workers' Compensation Appeals Board

31 East Channel Street, Rm. 344
Stockton, CA 95202-2393

Redding

Workers' Compensation Appeals Board

2115 Civic Center Drive , Suite 15
Redding, CA 96001-2796

Sacramento

Workers' Compensation Appeals Board

2424 Arden Way, Ste 230
Sacramento, CA 95825-2403

San Bernardino

Workers' Compensation Appeals Board

464 W. Fourth St., Ste 239
San Bernardino, CA 92401-1411

San Francisco

Workers' Compensation Appeals Board

455 Golden Gate Avenue, 2nd Floor
San Francisco, CA 94102-3660

Santa Ana

Worker's Compensation Appeals Board

28 Civic Center Plaza, Ste 451
Santa Ana, CA 92701-4070

Santa Rosa

Workers' Compensation Appeals Board

50 "D" Street, Ste 420
Santa Rosa, CA 95404-4760

Van Nuys

Workers' Compensation Appeals Board

6150 Van Nuys Blvd. Rm. 105
Van Nuys, CA 91401-3373

Things to Obtain in Case of an Accident on the Job

Accident Evidence Checklist

- Photograph accident scene
- Identify eyewitnesses
- Document names and contact info of witnesses
- Identify Subrogation
  - Was a piece of equipment involved
    - Get manufacturer and serial number
    - Secure the evidence
  - Was a third party involved
    - Get name, company, drivers license
    - Get contact info
    - Get insurance info
- Secure driver logs
- Copy of drivers license
- Create evidence list and send with accident report to your insurance carrier
- Keep copies for yourself
- Document, in diary form, ongoing claim issues

Notes:

Injury Illness Prevention Program Template

You may use this basic template to devise your own IIP program. Make it a point to devise such a program with a trained professional. Your insurance broker should be able to assist you. The most important aspect of your IIP is communication. Ensure that every employee, from the president of the company to the least of employees can understand and follow the plan!

Template

1. Overview

2. Program elements

3. Company IIP Policy

4. Scope of program

5. Purpose

6. Responsibilities

7. Program Elements

   o   Safety Communications

   o   Health and Safety Inspections

   o   Injury Reporting and Investigation

   o   Elimination and Correction of Workplace Hazards

- o Employee Safety Training

- o Documentation of Safety Conditions and Activities

- o Employee Access to Exposure and Medical Records

- o Hazard Control Programs, Policies, and Procedures

8. Compliance Checklists

(see Safety Checklists on next page)

Safety Checklists

Securing basic safety checklists

The Occupational Safety and Health Administration (OSHA) provide self inspection checklists for use by employers. They are a good foundation for developing your own Injury Illness Prevention Program. Please check the link below.

http://www.osha.gov/SLTC/smallbusiness/chklist.html#safety

Safety Training Information

OSHA maintains a Small Business Outreach Training Program which provides instructional material directed specifically at small business. You may obtain these materials via internet at the following link:

http://www.osha.gov/SLTC/smallbusiness/index.html

The materials provided are for training only and are not a substitute for OSHA regulations, however, the site provide excellent presentation materials to help devise a standout presentation!

Work Station Design Strategies

One of the major contributors to musculoskeletal disorders and injuries is poor work station design. Work stations should be designed to accommodate the person who actually works on a specific job. To design a workstation for the "average" person will result in a workstation that fits very few employees.

When designing a work station consider the following:

1. Arrange job duties so that people can work closer to their center of gravity (their stomach area)
2. Ensure that employees avoid using just one set of muscles on one side of their bodies. They should switch from left side to right.
3. Design conveyors, tables and workstations with enough room for employees to place their feet underneath.
4. Provide adjustable chairs and stools. Chairs should swivel and have adjustable backrests. The chairs should also be padded in the seat and in the armrests.
5. Provide footrests for employees who stand or sit.
6. Arrange work heights to be about 26 to 32 inches from the floor when working in a seated position.
7. Have employees alternate between sitting and standing positions if the work allows.

8. Design work stations so that employees can work with their wrists and elbows in a neutral position.

9. Avoid static work, or work that involves working in a set position for too long.

There are many other workstation tips that you can utilize to reduce the potential for injury on the job. Work station design should be a major element of your Injury Illness Prevention Program. Speak with your insurance carrier or insurance broker about workstation design.

Organizations to Consider

Public Agency Risk Managers Association (PARMA)

The Employers Group

Risk and Insurance Management Society (RIMS)

Professionals in Human Resources Association (PIHRA)

Look them up on the internet!

About the Authors

Gustavo L. Ortiz

Workers' Compensation Consultant

Gus began his workers compensation consulting practice in 1998. He specializes in claims administration, investigations, training and performance coaching. Gus has over 19 years of workers' compensation experience with major corporations including Great American West, Hartford, National American Insurance, California Compensation and AIG. He has worked with top management teams to develop and implement loss control plans, establish effective claims practices, implement fraud investigation programs, provide individual and management level coaching and refine reserves.

Gus holds a Bachelor of Arts degree in Communications from California State University Fullerton. He is a California State Certified Claims Administrator and a State certified insurance trainer.

Sean P. Nitzen, ARM
Workers' Compensation Consultant

Sean has over ten years of experience in workers' compensation with various size organizations including Crawford & Company, Scott Wetzel Services, Sullivan, Curtis, Monroe and Risk Enterprise Management/Zurich USA. He is IEA certified, a licensed California Claims Administrator and an Associate in Risk Management (ARM).

Sean has helped to implement effective claims practice procedures, streamline workflow processes and devise innovative methods to create significant cost reductions within many claims organizations. His strength in communications empowers him to effectively coach claims personnel of all levels and expertise.

Sean holds a Bachelor of Arts degree in Business Administration with an emphasis in Marketing with a minor in Economics

Sean holds a Bachelor of Arts degree in Business Administration with an emphasis in Marketing with a minor in Economics.

Look for future titles from G. Ortiz Productions & Publications:

Risk Manager's Guide to Employer Level Investigations

Workers Comp Claims Management Software for Employers

Human Resources Guide to Preventing Violence in the Workplace

Small Employer's Manual for WorkStation Design

To order bulk quantities of this book directly from the publisher please check out our website at:

www.gobookwriters.com

www.ingramcontent.com/pod-product-compliance
Lightning Source LLC
Chambersburg PA
CBHW022132170526
45157CB00004B/1854